I love ?

Written and compiled by Su Box
Illustrated by Hannah Firmin

LION

A Lion Book
an imprint of
Lion Hudson plc
Wilkinson House, Jordan Hill Road
Oxford OX2 8DR, England
www.lionhudson.com
ISBN 978 0 7459 5315 1

First edition 2009
10 9 8 7 6 5 4 3 2 1 0

Acknowledgments

All uncredited quotes written by Su Box.
pp. 17, 28 1 John 4:18, Song of Solomon 8:7 taken from the Holy Bible, New
International Version, copyright © 1973, 1978, 1984 International Bible Society.
Used by permission of Zondervan and Hodder & Stoughton Limited. All rights
reserved. The 'NIV' and 'New International Version' trademarks are registered
in the United States Patent and Trademark Office by International Bible Society.
Use of either trademark requires the permission of International Bible Society.
UK trademark number 1448790.
p. 29 1 Corinthians 13:7–8 taken from the New American Standard Bible®,
Copyright © 1960, 1962, 1963, 1968, 1971, 1972, 1973, 1975, 1977, 1995 by
The Lockman Foundation. Used by permission.

A catalogue record for this book is available
from the British Library

Typeset in Snell Roundhand
Printed and bound in Singapore

I couldn't help it 6

You make me laugh 10

You make me feel good 14

We're travelling through life together 18

You're irresistible 22

Our love is here to stay 26

I couldn't help it

*Love is something
you fall into.*
Barbara Kruger

*Falling in love consists
merely in uncorking the
imagination and bottling
the common sense.*
Helen Rowland

*A very small degree of hope is sufficient
to cause the birth of love.*
Stendhal

*Never frown, because you never know who
might be falling in love with your smile.*
Justine Milton

8

*It's easy to fall in love. The hard part
is finding someone to catch you.*

Bertrand Russell

*Trip over love, and you can get up.
Fall in love and you fall forever.*

Author unknown

*Love sought is good,
but given unsought is better.*

William Shakespeare

You make me laugh

Anyone can be passionate, but it takes real lovers to be silly.

Rose Franken

Love is when you tell a guy you like his shirt, then he wears it every day.

A child's definition of love

Fun is the fragrance of love.

Mike Yaconelli

On our first date I booked at a steak restaurant. On our second date I discovered you were a vegetarian.

*It ain't
because lovers
are so sensitive that they
quarrel so often; it is because there is so
much fun in making up.*

Josh Billings

*That's all anybody needs. To have love
in one hand and laughter in the other.*

August Wilson

*True love comes quietly, without
banners or flashing lights. If you hear
bells, get your ears checked.*

Erich Segal

13

You make me feel good

*I love you because you
encourage me to be who
I need to be.*

*I love you not only for what
you are, but for what I am
when I am with you.*

Roy Croft

*I love that I don't need to
pretend with you.
When you love someone,
you love him as he is.*

Charles Péguy

*What I think are
my imperfections you
say make me unique.*

*There is no fear in love. But perfect
love drives out fear.*

The Bible

*The consciousness of loving
and being loved brings a
warmth and richness to life
that nothing else can bring.*

Oscar Wilde

17

We're travelling through life together

Love does not consist of gazing at each other, but in looking together in the same direction.

Antoine de Saint-Exupéry

I love you because you know our relationship is a journey, not a destination.

Love is not the feeling of a moment but the conscious decision for a way of life.

Ulrich Schaffer

Just when I think I can read you like a book, you surprise me.

It is only with the heart that one can see rightly; what is essential is invisible to the eye.

Antoine de Saint-Exupéry

Love itself is what is left over when being in love has burned away…

Louis de Bernières (*Captain Corelli's Mandolin*)

Love is… when a minute apart seems like an hour, and an hour together flashes by.

The slowest kiss
makes too much haste.

Thomas Middleton

I love you soulfully and bodyfully,
properly and improperly, every way that
a woman can be loved.

George Bernard Shaw

You say you're not good with words —
but you can tell me you love me without
speaking.

Love is friendship set on fire.

Jeremy Taylor

All really great lovers are articulate,
and verbal seduction is the surest road to
actual seduction.

Marya Mannes

Sex is a conversation carried out by
other means.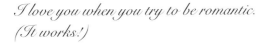

Peter Ustinov

I love you when you try to be romantic.
(It works!)

If love is blind, why is lingerie so
popular?

Author unknown

Our love is here to stay

Sustaining a loving relationship is like juggling. It looks easy until you try it.

Many waters cannot quench love; rivers cannot wash it away.

The Bible

You don't marry someone you can live with – you marry the person whom you cannot live without.

Author unknown

A successful marriage requires falling in love many times, always with the same person.

Mignon McLaughlin

Love bears all things,
believes all things, hopes
all things, endures all things.
Love never fails.

The Bible

True love doesn't have a happy ending.
True love doesn't have an ending.

Author unknown

I love you. And that's enough.

29